DAVIS-BACON: THE ACT AND THE LITERATURE

DAVIS-BACON: THE ACT AND THE LITERATURE

WILLIAM G. WHITTAKER

Novinka Books
New York

Senior Editors: Susan Boriotti and Donna Dennis
Coordinating Editor: Tatiana Shohov
Office Manager: Annette Hellinger
Graphics: Wanda Serrano
Editorial Production: Jennifer Vogt, Matthew Kozlowski and Maya Columbus
Circulation: Ave Maria Gonzalez, Indah Becker, Raymond Davis and Vladimir Klestov
Communications and Acquisitions: Serge P. Shohov
Marketing: Cathy DeGregory

Library of Congress Cataloging-in-Publication Data
Available Upon Request

ISBN 1-59033-375-6

Copyright © 2002 by Novinka Books, An Imprint of
Nova Science Publishers, Inc.
400 Oser Ave, Suite 1600
Hauppauge, New York 11788-3619
Tele. 631-231-7269   Fax 631-231-8175
e-mail: Novascience@earthlink.net
Web Site: http://www.novapublishers.com

All rights reserved. No part of this book may be reproduced, stored in a retrieval system or transmitted in any form or by any means: electronic, electrostatic, magnetic, tape, mechanical photocopying, recording or otherwise without permission from the publishers.

The authors and publisher have taken care in preparation of this book, but make no expressed or implied warranty of any kind and assume no responsibility for any errors or omissions. No liability is assumed for incidental or consequential damages in connection with or arising out of information contained in this book.

This publication is designed to provide accurate and authoritative information with regard to the subject matter covered herein. It is sold with the clear understanding that the publisher is not engaged in rendering legal or any other professional services. If legal or any other expert assistance is required, the services of a competent person should be sought. FROM A DECLARATION OF PARTICIPANTS JOINTLY ADOPTED BY A COMMITTEE OF THE AMERICAN BAR ASSOCIATION AND A COMMITTEE OF PUBLISHERS.

Printed in the United States of America

CONTENTS

Preface		vii
Introduction		ix
Chapter 1	The Davis-Bacon Act of 1931 (As Amended)	1
	Origins of the Act	1
	A Gradual Process of Evolution	3
	Early Modification	3
	A Period of Growing Contentiousness	5
Chapter 2	Getting to Know the Davis-Bacon Act, Pro and Con	11
	Arguments Generally Critical of Davis-Bacon	11
	Arguments Generally Supportive of Davis-Bacon	12
Chapter 3	How Good is the Information We Have Concerning the Effects of the Davis-Bacon Act?	15
	The General Nature of Davis-Bacon Research	16
	Significant Gaps	17
	Some Agency Studies	17
	Views from the Private Sector	18
Bibliography		23
Index		39

PREFACE

The Davis-Bacon Act of 1931, as amended, requires that contractors, engaging in certain federal contract construction, pay workers on such projects not less than the locally prevailing wage for comparable work. In addition, such contractors are required to file payroll reports and to meet other administrative and labor standards requirements.

Enacted at the urging of the Hoover Administration, the statute was modified in 1934 with adoption of the Copeland ("anti-kickback") Act and in 1935 through general amendments dealing with administration and implementation: among them, establishment of a $2,000 coverage threshold (the threshold had been $5,000 in the original enactment), a requirement that the prevailing wage rate be determined prior to submission of bids, and extension of coverage both to public buildings and public works including painting and decorating. In 1964, the concept of "prevailing wage" was expanded to include a fringe benefit component. The statute has also been the subject of technical amendments through the years and Davis-Bacon provisions have been added to more than 50 federal program statutes.

The Act contains a provision allowing for its suspension by the president of the United States during a "national emergency." It has been suspended on three occasions: in 1934 by President Roosevelt, in 1971 by President Nixon, and in 1992 by President Bush. In each instance, the suspension was brief and the Act was subsequently restored to its full strength.

While there is a relatively extensive literature (both popular and scholarly) concerning the Act, there also appear to be significant gaps in our knowledge of the statute and its impact. Some have questioned the adequacy of the data upon which analysis of Davis-Bacon impact rests. During the

Reagan Administration, changes were instituted in the manner in which the Act was implemented and these, in turn, have produced a need for further, more current, data for analytical purposes.

Included, here, is a select bibliography of published materials dealing with the Davis-Bacon Act and immediately related issues. The list includes popular and scholarly sources but does not include an inventory of congressional documents, agency reports or, for the most part, publications of interest groups.

INTRODUCTION

The Davis-Bacon Act (40 U.S. C. 276a-276A-5) became law in 1931. As amended, the Act requires that construction contracts entered into by the federal government specify minimum wages to be paid to the various classes of laborers and mechanics working under those contracts.[1] Minimum wages are defined by the Act as those determined by the Secretary of Labor (a) to be prevailing (b) in the locality of the project (c) for similar crafts and skills (d) on comparable construction work. The prevailing wage concept was expanded in 1964 to include a fringe benefit component. The Act has a coverage threshold of $2,000.

Through the years, Davis-Bacon prevailing wage provisions have been added to more than 50 program statutes. In addition, many states and some local jurisdictions have "little Davis-Bacon" acts of their own. Most of these differ from each other in coverage or other requirements – and differ, as well, from the federal statute.

This book sketches the evolution of the Davis-Bacon Act and suggests the scope of the controversy that has formed around it. It then examines, briefly, some of the trends in the scholarship and reportage concerning the Act and, finally, provides a bibliography of published non-documentary sources that are generally available to persons with a deeper interest in the statute, its history, and its administration.

---

[1] Alongside the Davis-Bacon Act are two other, different, statutes governing labor standards in federal contracts for goods and services respectively: The Walsh-Healey Act (1936), 41 U.S.C. 35-45; and the McNamara-O'Hara Service Contract Act (1965), 41 U.S. C. 351-358. These laws are supplemented by other federal statutes that deal with hours of work and health and safety standards.

Chapter 1

THE DAVIS-BACON ACT OF 1931 (AS AMENDED)

Early in the 20th century, it was not at all clear that the federal government had the authority to regulate wages and conditions of work in the private sector.[1] When Congress attempted to deal legislatively with hours of work, child labor or minimum wages, its enactments were often found by the courts to be in violation of its constitutional authority. Only after 1937 when the U.S. Supreme Court sustained a Washington State labor standards statute (*West Coast Hotel v. Parrish* (300 U.S. 379)) did Congress assume a more confident affirmative role in regulation of the workplace.[2]

ORIGINS OF THE ACT

If government found its role in the private sector somewhat circumscribed by the courts, it was on firmer constitutional ground in

---

[1] About this period, see: Bernstein, Irving. *The Lean years: A History of the American Worker, 1920-1933*. Boston, Houghton Mifflin, 1960; Brandeis, Louis D. The Constitution and the Minimum Wage. *The Survey*, February 6, 1915. p. 490-494, 521-524; Zieger, Robert H. *Republicans and Labor, 1919-1929*. Lexington, KY., University of Kentucky Press, 1969; and Mitchell, Broadus. *Depression Decade: From New Era Through New Deal, 1929-1941*. New York, Rinehard & Company, Inc., 1960.

[2] Chambers, John W. The Big Switch: Justice Roberts and the Minimum Wage Cases. *Labor History*, winter 1969. p. 44-73. The Fair Labor Standards Act, the basic federal statute dealing with minimum wages, overtime pay and child labor, was enacted in 1938 – 7 years after Davis-Bacon became law.

prescribing labor standards for its own direct employees.[3] Thus, public employees, both federal and those in state and local government, were often protected by mandated minimum wage and overtime pay standards. But, while their own employees were protected, some public agencies sought to circumvent these requirements (and to expand their purchasing power) by "contracting out" for construction, goods and services. This caused some reformers to protest that the various units of government ought to provide a better example of fairness for private sector employers.

In 1891, Kansas adopted a law requiring that "not less than the current rate of *per diem* wages in the locality where the work is performed shall be paid to laborers, workmen, mechanics, and other persons so employed by or on behalf of the state of Kansas" or of other local jurisdictions. Through the next several decades, other states followed suit, enacting a variety of labor-protective statutes covering workers in contract production.[4]

Federal contracting practice, into the 1930s, required that "the lowest responsible bid" be accepted. In this instance, responsibility referred to a reasonable expectation that a project could be completed in a timely fashion without regard for the wages paid to workers or the conditions under which they worked. This "made the government an unwilling collaborator with unscrupulous firms that sought to get government business by cutting wages."[5] In the construction field, it was alleged that migratory contractors from low-wage sections of the country would bid for federal work and, because they paid wage rates lower than those prevailing in the locality of a proposed project (and employed nonresident workers), they enjoyed a competitive advantage over "fair" local contractors.

In 1927, Representative Robert L. Bacon (R-N.Y.) introduced legislation to require that locally prevailing wage standards be met in federal construction work. Although hearings were conducted, the legislation was not brought to the floor. Similar legislation was introduced in 1928 and again in 1930. Finally, in March 1931, at the urging of the Hoover Administration, the Bacon Act (co-sponsored by Senator James Davis (R-Pa.), formerly

---

[3] Concerning early labor standards protections for public employees, see: Cahill, Marion Cotter. *Shorter Hours: A Study of the Movement Since the Civil War*. New York, Columbia University Press, 1932; Fine, Sidney. The Eight-Hour Day Movement in the United States, 1999-1891. *The Mississippi Valley Historical Review*, December 1953. p. 441-462; and, Kelly, Matthew A. Early Federal Regulation of Hours of Labor in the United States. *Industrial and Labor Relations Review*, April 1950. p. 362-374.
[4] Johnson, David B. Prevailing Wage Legislation in the States. *Monthly Labor Review*, August 1, 1991. p. 839-845.
[5] Morton, Herbert C. *Public Contracts and Private Wages: Experience Under the Walsh-Healey Act*. Washington, The Brookings Institution, 1965. p. 8.

Secretary of Labor in the Harding, Coolidge and Hoover Administrations) was passed and signed by President Herbert Hoover.

A GRADUAL PROCESS OF EVOLUTION[6]

Almost immediately after its adoption, certain deficiencies in the Davis-Bacon Act became apparent. Both industry and organized labor, while voicing different concerns, appealed to the Congress and to the White House for revision of the statute.

Early Modification

While mandating under Davis-Bacon that not less than the locally prevailing wage be paid, Congress had not established a regular system through which such wage rate determinations might be made. Thus, contractors, when bidding on a public project, had to commit themselves to pay whatever wage could be agreed upon or, in the event of a dispute whatever wage the Secretary of Labor might later decide was prevailing. Thus, industry sought amendment of the Act to provide for *predetermination* of wage rates.

Organized labor was concerned that enforcement procedures under the Act were inadequate. Pointing to the $5,000 threshold for triggering the statute, it noted that certain employers might fragment contracts in order to escape the Act's requirements. Besides, the unions suggested, many contracts for painting and decorating fell below the threshold and thus, workers in those fields would not be covered at all.[7]

It was alleged that some employers paid the locally prevailing rate to their employees as the Act required, but would then demand, under the table, a "kick-back" of a portion of that wage. Some estimated that as much as 25% of the legitimate wage costs for federal projects was being returned to employers through kick-back arrangements.[8]

---

[6] A more extensive historical overview of the Act appears in: CRS Report 94-408, *The Davis-Bacon Act: Institutional Evolution and Public Policy*, by William G. Whittaker.

[7] Thieblot, Armand J., Jr. *The Davis-Bacon Act*. Philadelphia, The Wharton School, University of Pennsylvania, 1975. p. 11.

[8] U.S. Congress. Senate. Subcommittee of the Committee on Education and labor. *Investigation of the Relationship Existing Between Certain Contractors and Their Employees in the*

Executive Order No. 5778 (1932

Under pressure both from labor and employers, Congress commenced oversight hearings on the recently adopted statute in January 1932; but, just as the hearings began, President Hoover issued Executive order No. 4778, generally strengthening the enforcement and administration of the Act.[9] Since the Hoover reforms, a fine tuning of implementation of the statute, had been achieved through administrative action and, thus, could be reversed at will by a later President, Congress pressed forward with legislative action.[10] But, when the legislation reached the President's desk in July 1932, Mr. Hoover vetoed the bill, his Labor Secretary, William Doak, observing that the measure "would be impracticable of administration" and "would stretch a new bureaucracy across the country."[11]

The Copeland "Anti-Kickback" Act (1934)

Congressional hearings on public contracting issues continued through the next several years. With support from the Roosevelt Administration, legislation authored by Senator Royal Copeland (D-N.Y.) was called up in the Senate (April 26, 1934) and, after a brief statement by the Senator, passed.[12] The House proceeded in a similar fashion, acting without debate. On June 13, 1934, President Franklin Roosevelt signed the measure. The Copeland "anti-kickback" Act provided a fine and/or imprisonment for anyone who induces any person engaged in federal or federally financed construction "to give up any part of the compensation to which he is entitled under his contract of employment." The Act authorized the administering agencies to "make reasonable regulations" for its enforcement, but specifically required that "each contractor and subcontractor shall furnish weekly a sworn affidavit with respect to the wages paid each employee during the preceding week."[13]

United States. Hearings on S.Res. 228. 73d Cong., 2d Sess., Part 1, May 4, 7, and June 21, 22 and 23, 1934. Washington, U.S. Govt. Print. Off., 1934. p. 3.

[9] U.S. President (Hoover). *Executive Orders, 5735-6070*, October 1931 – March 1933. Collected set, bound by the Library of Congress.

[10] *Congressional Record*, June 8, 1932. p. 12363-12390, and June 20, 1932, p. 13471.

[11] *Public Papers of the Presidents of the United States: Herbert Hoover, 1932-1933.* Washington, U.S. Govt. Print. Off., 1977. p. 286.

[12] *Congressional Record*, April 26, 1934. p. 7401.

[13] *Congressional Record*, June 7, 1934. p. 10759.

The Davis-Bacon Amendments of 1935

By the spring of 1935, Senator David Walsh (D-Mass.) had drawn up general Davis-Bacon amendments, designed to address perceived administrative problems. The Davis-Bacon amendments of 1935 reduced the threshold for coverage from $5,000 to $2,000. They provided coverage for all federal contract construction of whatever character to which the United States and the District of Columbia might be a party: "construction, alternation, and/or repair, including painting and decorating, or public buildings or public works." Henceforth, bids for contracts covered by Davis-Bacon were to state "the minimum wages to be paid various classes of laborers and mechanics," thus establishing a requirement of *predetermination* of the wage rates. The Comptroller General was directed to prepare a list of contractors who had "disregarded their obligations to employees and subcontractors" with such violators of the Davis-Bacon/Copeland provisions to suffer potential debarment from further federal contracts for a period of up to 3 years. Other administrative provisions were also included.[14]

A Period of Growing Contentiousness

For a period of about 20 years following adoption of the 1935 Davis-Bacon Act amendments, the Act appears to have attracted little attention.[15] Then, in the mid-1950s, Congress began, increasingly, to add Davis-Bacon provisions to program statutes, triggering debate over both the substance and application of the Act.[16] Defense construction and the new space program brought the Act into renewed prominence during the early 1960s and, since that time, it has remained more-or-less continuously a focus of congressional interest.

---

[14] *Congressional Record*, July 30, 1935, p. 12073-12074; August 23, 1935, p. 14384; and, August 30, 1935, p. 14753. See also: U.S. Congress. House. Committee on Labor. *Amend the Act Approved March 3, 1931, Relating to Rate of Wages for Laborers and Mechanics Employed on Public Buildings*. Report to Accompany S. 3303, August 9, 1935. Washington, U.S. Govt. Print. Off., 1935. p. 1.

[15] Letter to Leaders of Labor and Management in the Building and Construction Industry. *Public Papers of the presidents of the United States: Harry S. Truman, January 1 to December 31, 1947*. Washington, U.S. Govt. print. Off., 1963. p. 117-118.

[16] U.S. Congress. House. Committee on Public Works. *Federal Highway and Highway Revenue Acts of 1956*. Report to Accompany H.R. 10660. House Report No. 2022, 84th Cong., 2d Sess. Washington, U.S. Govt. Print. Off., 1971. p. 13.

The Roosevelt Subcommittee (1962-1964)

In 1962, a Special Subcommittee of the House Committee on Education and Labor was assigned the task of general oversight of Davis-Bacon Act – by this point, 3 decades old – and the related contract labor standards statutes. Chaired by Representative James Roosevelt (D-Ca.), the Subcommittee conducted the most extensive review of the Act since the mid-1930s.

In addition to general operation of the statute, the Roosevelt Subcommittee focused specifically upon the following areas: (a) how Davis-Bacon wage rate determinations are made and the extent to which they are an accurate reflection of wage rates that actually prevail, locally, in the area of construction; (b) whether a system of review of Davis-Bacon wage rate determinations and related decisions of the Department of Labor might be needed; and (c) "any other constructive proposals" for the improvement of the Act and of its administration.[17] The work of the Subcommittee resulted in enactment of the 1964 "fringe benefit" amendment to the Act which expanded the prevailing rate concept from the cash wage alone to both cash and fringe benefits – of the value of the latter.[18] Further, indirectly, it may have encouraged the Secretary of Labor, Willard Wirtz, to create within the Department in 1964 the Wage appeals Board to hear Davis-Bacon cases.[19] But, there were no broad changes in the Act comparable to those of 1935.

The Subcommittee, however, exposed what appears to have been a jurisdictional clash between the General Accounting Office (GAO) and the Department of Labor (DOL) with respect to Davis-Bacon. Spokespersons for GAO, testifying before the Subcommittee, were openly critical of the Department's administration of the Act.[20] In the wake of the hearings, there followed, between 1962 and 1971, a series of eight separate GAO reports that urged reform of the administration of the Act and that seemed to argue that Davis-Bacon might be ill-advised as public policy. How seriously GAO's perspectives were taken is not entirely clear, but Congress continued to support the Act and to extend its provisions as various construction-related measures were adopted.

---

[17] U.S. Congress. House. Committee on Education and Labor. Special Subcommittee on Labor. *Administration of the Davis-Bacon Act.* Hearings. 87th Cong., 2d Sess. Part I, June 6, 7, 8, 11 and 12, 1961. Washington, U.S. Govt. Print. Off., 1962. p. 1. (hereafter cited as House Subcommittee on labor, *Administration of the Davis-Bacon Act*.)

[18] *Congressional Quarterly Almanac*, 1964. Congressional Quarterly, Inc., Washington, 1965. p. 576-577.

[19] *Federal Register*. January 4, 1964. p. 118-119.

[20] House Subcommittee on labor, *Administration of the Davis-Bacon Act*, p. 183-284, 319-322, and 325-454.

The Nixon Suspension of Davis-Bacon (1971)

The authors of the Davis-Bacon, in 1931, had included a provision which allows the President, "[i]n the event of a national emergency," to suspend the Act. The concept of "national emergency" was not defined nor were the conditions under which a suspension might occur. In 1934, President Franklin Roosevelt had suspended the Act *for 3 weeks*, apparently for purposes of administrative convenience related to operation of the various New Deal enactments of that period. The Nixon suspension of Davis-Bacon (1971) occurred within the context of the President's campaign to bring inflation under control.

In 1970, President Richard Nixon was engaged in an effort to curb inflationary pressures – notably within the construction industry. He had conferred both with industry and trade union officials urging moderation in wage/price matters but, apparently, without entire success. In that context, on February 23, 1971, President Nixon suspended the Davis-Bacon Act and suspended, as well, the Davis-Bacon provisions that had been incorporated by Congress in the various federal program statutes. His action raised a number of issues, some of them legal, and gave the Davis-Bacon Act renewed visibility. A month later, on March 29, 1971, the President restored the Act, unchanged, but also established a tripartite Construction Industry Stabilization Committee as part of his wage/price control apparatus.[21]

Administrative Clash over Davis-Bacon

Through the 1970s, administrative conflict over Davis-Bacon (and efforts to reform or to repeal the Act) grew more intense. With the diverse character of federal programs (in construction, goods and services), a need arose for better operational coordination of various statutes and regulations, among them the federal contract labor standards statutes. In reorganization plans set forth in 1947 and 1950, the Truman Administration had attempted to establish, clearly, responsibility for administration of the Davis-Bacon Act; but that initiative notwithstanding, interagency disputes with respect to Davis-Bacon (and the related Walsh-Healey and McNamara-O'Hara Acts) appear to have continued.

During the Ford and Carter Administrations, these interagency disputes continued intermittently, involving the Department of Labor, the several

---

[21] CRS Report 79-249, *The Davis-Bacon Act Suspension of 1971: The Nixon Administration, Organized Labor and the Prevailing Wage Statute in Federal and Federally Assisted Construction*, by William G. Whittaker.

contracting agencies, the Office of Management and Budget, and GAO. Further, interest groups, journalists and political pundits lined up on each side of these conflicts – and, ultimately, these matters, essentially administrative, became the focus of congressional hearings. In turn, the hearings generated further public comment and reaction both from defenders and from critics of the Act.

The 1979 GAO Report

Amid interagency squabbles and industry criticism of the Act, a new report appeared from the General Accounting Office. The 1979 GAO report was titled simply, *The Davis-Bacon Act Should Be Repealed*.[22] Immediately controversial, the report reviewed GAO's longstanding criticism of the DOL's administration of the Act. Through the summer of 1979, the report and the issues it raised became the focus of three congressional hearings – though no legislated revision of the Act was passed. Perhaps as important as legislation, however, the GAO report (with the hearings record) provided a body of material from which critics of the Act would draw through the next decade and beyond.

Influenced in part by the GAO report and by the attention that it had focused upon Davis-Bacon issues, the DOL (late in the Carter Administration) proposed certain changes in the administration of the Act. But, in practical terms, these proposals came too late. Published on January 16, 1981, they would have taken effect on February 14, 1981 – by which point a new Presidential administration had assumed control. The proposals for reform of the Davis-Bacon Act, issued by the Carter Administration, were promptly withdrawn by President Reagan.[23]

Administrative Reform under President Reagan

Building from the foundation laid down by the Carter Administration, the Reagan Labor Department proposed a new body of Davis-Bacon reforms in August 1971, calling for public comment.[24] Final regulations were issued in May 1982 to take effect in July of that year. Labor Secretary Raymond Donovan affirmed that "the final rule should be very well received by contractor groups." He also acknowledged that "labor may react

---

[22] U.S. General Accounting Office. *The Davis-Bacon Act Should Be Repealed*. Report to the Congress by the Comptroller General of the United States. HRD-79-18, April 27, 1979. 115 p. (Hereafter cited as GAO, *The Davis-Bacon Act Should Be Repealed*).

[23] *Federal Register*, December 28, 1979. p. 77026; and January 16, 1981, p. 4306.

[24] *Federal Register*, August 13, 1981. p. 41428.

unfavorably."²⁵ He was right on both counts. Trade union leaders were "shocked and angered" and viewed the regulations as a "back door attempt to nullify the law."²⁶ Industry sources, noting that they had been "working for years to abolish or amend the Davis-Bacon law and the regulations that implement it" termed the Reagan regulations "a major improvement."²⁷

Essentially, the Reagan regulations simplified the wage rate determination procedures, weakened or streamlined (depending upon one's perspective) the reporting requirements of the Copeland "anti-kickback" Act, and would have allowed increased flexibility in the employment of "helpers" (persons not necessarily possessing craft training) on Davis-Bacon projects. Litigation extended into the Bush Administration. At large, the courts acceded to the Secretary of Labor's discretion in wage rate determination. However, the Department was instructed to restructure its Copeland Act proposals and those dealing with the use of helpers. That process has not yet resulted in final regulatory change. Meanwhile, some have argued that the Reagan reforms, like those instituted by President Hoover 50 years earlier, are vulnerable to further change, administratively, and therefore ought to be codified in statute.²⁸

The Bush Suspension of Davis-Bacon (1992-1993)

Davis-Bacon critics had, through the years and for a variety of reasons, urged that the Act be suspended by Presidential decree – as the President has the authority to do within the context of a "national emergency." During the winter and spring of 1992, that action was urged upon George Bush but, by early summer, the issue had faded from public view.

Then, on October 14, 1992, President Bush suspended Davis-Bacon as applied in parts of the states of Florida, Louisiana and Hawaii. The three states had been battered by hurricanes and President Bush declared the resulting destruction *an emergency* for purposes of suspending Davis-Bacon.²⁹ The suspension, he affirmed, could create "as many as five to eleven thousand new jobs in the construction industry in these states" and he

---

[25] Bureau of National Affairs. *Daily Labor Report*, May 28, 1982. p. A6. (Hereafter cited as *DLR*).
[26] *DLR*, May 27, 1982. p. A1 and F1.
[27] *Washington Report*. United States Chamber of Commerce, June 8, 1982. p. 1 and 20.
[28] See U.S. Library of Congress. Congressional Research Service. *Davis-Bacon Act and New Department of labor Regulations*. Typed report by Vincent Treacy. January 18, 1985. 6 p.
[29] Proclamation 6491, reproduced in *Weekly Compilation of Presidential Documents*, v. 28, no. 42, October 19, 1992. p. 1936-1937.

noted further that payment of the locally prevailing wage in the storm-damaged areas would "increase the costs" of rebuilding. Critics argued that the suspension was not justified. The suspension was open-ended – to remain in effect until President Bush or his successor restored the Act.[30] On March 6, 1993, President William Clinton did restore the statute to its full force.[31]

Because of the difficulty of collecting relevant data, it would have been necessary to have had a plan for such collection in place at the time of the 1992-1993 suspension. Since this apparently was not done, there is no available comprehensive assessment of the impact, if any, of the suspension.

---

[30] The White House. Office of the Press Secretary. Press Release. *Emergency Suspension of the Davis-Bacon Act.* October 14, 1992. 2 p.

[31] Presidential Proclamation No. 6534. *Federal Register*, March 10, 1993. p. 13189.

Chapter 2

GETTING TO KNOW THE DAVIS-BACON ACT, PRO AND CON

Through the years, arguments for and against Davis-Bacon have become largely fixed – as have the counter-arguments of defenders and critics. The logic and many of the assumptions that these arguments contain have been questioned at length. In the evolving debate, few contentions about the Act have gone (or are likely to go) unchallenged.

ARGUMENTS GENERALLY CRITICAL OF DAVIS-BACON

Some critics of Davis-Bacon argue, *inter alia*, that the Act has an inflationary impact (unnecessarily increasing the cost of federal construction), and that it hampers competition – especially with respect to small and minority-owned businesses unfamiliar with federal contracting procedures. They contend that it impedes efficient utilization of manpower, limiting the use of "helpers" or general utility workers. Some argue, were Davis-Bacon restrictions absent, that contractors would employ more minority and women workers because they can hire them more cheaply and, by fragmenting the tasks to be performed, use them as substitutes for more broadly skilled workers. Implicit, here, is the assumption that if employers are forced by Davis-Bacon to pay not less than the locally prevailing wage in a craft, they will hire more broadly skilled, highly trained, or experienced workers.

Besides, critics note, Congress has provided a general minimum wage floor with enactment of the Fair Labor Standards Act (1938). They argue that a "super minimum wage" for federal construction work is both unnecessary and unjust. They assert that labor costs for federal construction could be reduced (with savings for the taxpayer) if *actual* local market wages were paid rather than administratively determined locally prevailing wages (often the union rate, some argue). In addition, they urge simplification of the Copeland Act reporting requirements and of the compliance and wage rate determination process.

ARGUMENTS GENERALLY SUPPORTIVE OF DAVIS-BACON

Supporters of Davis-Bacon hold that the Act prevents cutthroat competition from "fly-by-night" firms that undercut local wages and working conditions and compete "unfairly" with local contractors: that the Act helps stabilize the local construction industry, an advantage to workers and employers alike. The Act, they suggest, may tend to assure the consuming agency of higher quality work since employers who are required to pay at least the locally prevailing wage are likely to hire more competent and productive workers – resulting in better workmanship, less waste, reduced need for supervision, and fewer mistakes requiring corrective action. This may lead to fewer cost overruns and more timely completion of public construction – and, in the long-term, lower rehabilitation and repair needs down the line. Thus, some argue, the Davis-Bacon Act could actually save the taxpayer money on public construction.

Supporters of the Act also argue that Davis-Bacon deters contractors from fragmenting construction tasks to utilize low-wage (and often low-skill) "helpers" or pick-up crews. They believe this could result in a trade-off of long-term social benefits for short-term profits. Some argue that without Davis-Bacon (and in the absence of a collective bargaining agreement), contractors would be unlikely to provide training, whether formally through a certified program or through informal investment in human capital (improving the skills of their regular employees). Advocates also contend that repeal or weakening of the Act may adversely affect apprenticeship programs in the construction industry to the disadvantage of minority and women workers who are entering the building trades in growing numbers. If "helpers" are substituted for skilled craft workers, it would likely be minorities (and, to a lesser extent, women) who would be laid off or forced into lower-wage jobs, some assert.

Chapter 3

HOW GOOD IS THE INFORMATION WE HAVE CONCERNING THE EFFECTS OF THE DAVIS-BACON ACT?

The Davis-Bacon Act, among labor laws, is *widely known* but it may not be *well known*. The Davis-Bacon literature, if one takes into account agency reports and congressional hearings, is extensive. These public documents have provided a basis both for popular and scholarly consideration of the Act.

Perhaps the most frequently asked question concerning the Davis-Bacon Act is: Would we save money if the Davis-Bacon Act were repealed or modified to narrow its scope? The short answer is: No one really knows. Conversely, might Davis-Bacon result in savings to the federal government in its purchases of construction? That, too, would seem to be an open question.

Another question frequently asked by those, both in industry and in the workforce, who may have to deal with the Davis-Bacon Act is: Is this particular project covered? And further: If so, why? If not, why not? To whom is assigned the judgment for making such determinations? Such questions might be answered were there a scholarly, institutional history of the Act and of its place within the broader field of public contracting policy. if such a study exists, it does not appear to be generally available.

The General Nature of Davis-Bacon Research

There have been numerous hearings through the 66 years since the Davis-Bacon legislation was first considered. They have tended to focus on policy issues or have served as a forum for airing complaints. Less time has been devoted to examination of economic impact or to its assessment.

The Davis-Bacon literature is extensive and diverse. Generally, it falls into three categories: public materials, i.e., agency reports and analyses; journalistic pieces; and academic studies. The latter are also diverse: work commissioned by interest groups (which may be scholarly, nonetheless), articles that merge journalism with scholarship, and putatively independent academic work.

Given the number of projects covered by the Act, it is nearly impossible for an independent scholar to review its administration and to assess its impact. *First.* There is the scope of the task: thousands of projects throughout the United States, administered by different agencies and involving hundreds of contractors. *Second.* There is the problem of availability of basic documentation. How much information has actually been preserved? Are the reports, required under the Copeland Act, factual and complete? Access to data presents a *third* problem. Assuming that the data are available, securing such documentation (and access to administrative personnel) may be problematic.

If one assumes that documentation exists, that the independent analyst is granted access to it, that all of the parties are cooperative, and that the means, financial and other, are available for such an undertaking, the analyst is left with a *fourth* complication. *He is comparing something that did happen with something that in fact, for whatever reasons, did not happen.* In the absence of a Davis-Bacon requirement, would the contract have gone to the same contractor? If so (or if not), would it have been managed in the same way? Did the contracting agency monitor the project carefully – and was such monitoring comparable with that for non Davis-Bacon projects? Did the Act have any impact upon the wages *actually* paid or upon workforce utilization? Without Davis-Bacon, would different workers have been employed?

These same questions confront a public agency in its efforts to investigate Aimpact: the availability of the data, the willingness of the various parties to cooperate in an investigation, and the speculative character of the comparison between what did happen, what did not happen, and what might or might not have happened under different circumstances. For a public agency, the task is no less massive than for a private scholar. And, in the public sector, there may be other constraints. How much funding and staff time should be devoted to an investigation of Davis-Bacon impact? What political or policy concerns may come into play?

SIGNIFICANT GAPS

There appear to be significant gaps in our knowledge of the Act and of its administration despite oversight by Congress, extensive study by public and private agencies, and the work of individual scholars. Further, few studies of the Act, whether public or private, have escaped criticism on the grounds of flawed methodology or inadequate sample size.

Some Agency Studies

Federal agency reports provide primary documentation concerning the Davis-Bacon Act. But often the various agencies have disagreed about assessment methodologies – sometimes, as in the 1970s, vigorously.

The General Accounting office, as might be expected, has conducted extensive oversight of the Act. During 1962 to 1971 alone, GAO issued eight reports, increasingly critical both of the statute and of its administration by the Department of Labor. In 1979, as noted above, it published an extensive analysis titled simply, *Davis-Bacon Should Be Repealed*. the 1979 GAO report was immediately controversial – and frequently cited. Labor Secretary Ray Marshall severely attacked the report, maintaining that it had "little credibility."[1] Subsequently, the report and the issues it raised were a focus of review by three separate congressional committees during which both its methodology and findings were questioned.[2]

The Congressional Budget Office (CBO) is frequently cited with respect to Davis-Bacon impact. In a 1983 report, *Modifying the Davis-Bacon Act: Implications for the Labor Market and the Federal Budget*, CBO attempted

---

[1] *Press Briefing by Secretary of Labor F. Ray Marshall*, July 17, 1979. p. 44 (A mimeographed press release.)
[2] See: U.S. Congress. House. Committee on Education and Labor. Subcommittee on Labor Standards. *Oversight Hearings on the Davis-Bacon Act*. 96th Cong., 1st Sess. Washington, U.S. Govt. Print. Off., 1979; U.S. Congress. Senate. Committee on Banking, Housing, and Urban Affairs. Subcommittee on Housing and Urban Affairs. *Davis-Bacon Legislation*. Hearing, 96th Cong., 1st Sess., May 2, 1979. Washington, U.S. Govt. Print. Off., 1979; and, U.S. Congress. Senate. Committee on Labor and Human Relations. *Military Construction Authorization Act, 1980*. Hearings, 96th Cong., 1st Sess. July 17 and 19, 1979. Washington, U.S. Govt. Print. Off., 1979.

to set a dollar figure for any increased cost of federal construction sparked by Davis-Bacon requirements. Cautiously, CBO noted "a number of problems in [the] available data and method" and noted that "data on these effects are highly inconclusive." CBO does not appear to have conducted independent research for its 1983 report, relying upon the existing literature which estimated a range of impact "from $75 million to $1 billion a year."[3]

A decade later, in his May 4, 1993, testimony before the House Subcommittee on Labor Standards, CBO Director Robert D. Reischauer noted: "Let me at this point mention a caveat about CBO's estimates, and this is that they are based on relatively old information. They are derived from a 1983 report that CBO issued that weighed the evidence from all off the studies that were available at that time. "Unfortunately," he added, "little has been written about the impact of the Davis-Bacon Act since 1983, and so we have had no reason to adjust our estimates."[4]

Both the 1979 GAO report and the 1983 CBO report (which still provide a basis for many Davis-Bacon impact estimates) are now dated. The Reagan Administration regulations governing administration of the Act, issued in the early 1980s, were proffered as a means through which to render implementation more efficient and to eliminate unnecessary costs. Parts of these reforms have been given effect, gradually, through the past decade. Thus, whatever the merit of GAO's findings in 1979 and the CBO's analysis in 1983, they may no longer be valid. New research, taking into account the effect of the Reagan reforms, may be needed.

Views from the Private Sector

The first question to ask when assessing Davis-Bacon literature is: What is the data of the data upon which it is based? If the data are from the pre-Reagan era (as most are), then the resultant studies may be of little use for current economic or policy analysis – the rules for implementation of the Act having been changed during that period and, thus, presumably, the cost impact of the statute.

---

[3] U.S. Congressional Budget Office. *Modifying the Davis-Bacon Act: Implications for the Labor Market and the Federal Budget.* Washington, U.S. Govt. Print. Off., 1983, p. xii and 26. See also Wisniewski, Stanley C. *A Preliminary Review of Congressional Budget Office (CBO) Cost Estimates of the Davis-Bacon Act.* Washington, Workplace Economics, Inc., 1986. 20 p.

[4] U.S. Congress. House. Committee on Education and Labor. Subcommittee on Labor Standards, Occupational Health and Safety. *Hearing on H.R. 1231: The Davis-Bacon Reform Bill of 1993.* 103d Cong., 1st Sess. Washington, U.S. Govt. Print. Off., 1993. p. 35-37, 49-51.

For many years, virtually the only major study of the statute was Armand Thieblot's 1975 monograph, *The Davis-Bacon Act*. Funded in part by the U.S. Chamber of Commerce and published by The Wharton School of the University of Pennsylvania, it is strongly critical of the Act. Thieblot concluded that the Act "makes little sense under conditions of prosperity and expansion and provides far too few benefits to offset its immense costs."[5] Thieblot's work was updated in 1986 – but appears to rely upon pre-Reagan data.

What is Thieblot's impact assessment for Davis-Bacon? He noes, broadening the range used by CBO, that "Davis-Bacon impact estimates have been presented during the past 10 years ranging from less than $50 million to more than $2 billion." While he suggests "there is no direct way to measure the Davis-Bacon impact,"[6] still, for his own part, he asserts: Davis-Bacon "costs more to operate than the whole federal judiciary establishment, and perhaps more to run than the entire legislative branch of government."[7] The basis for this assertion, however, is unclear.

Since 1980, Steven Allen has produced a number of studies that deal, directly or indirectly, with Davis-Bacon. In an essay with David Reich, *Prevailing Wage Laws Are Not Inflationary*, they argue that "there is strong evidence to suggest that there are significant productivity differences between low-wage and high-wage workers." Allen and Reich state: "Paying at least the locally prevailing wage rate will make it possible to attract better trained and more highly skilled construction workers able to complete the job quickly and efficiently." Focusing upon state experience, they conclude that "once all the relevant variables are taken into consideration, there is no evidence whatsoever of any correlation between the level of construction costs and the presence or absence of a state 'little Davis-Bacon Act.'"[8] The essay was prepared for the Center to Protect Workers' Rights, chaired by Robert Georgine, President of the Building and Construction Trades

---

[5] Thieblot, Armand J., Jr. *The Davis-Bacon Act*. The Wharton School, University of Pennsylvania, 1975. Mimeograph. p. 179. (Hereafter cited as Thieblot, *The Davis-Bacon Act*.)
[6] Thieblot, Armand J., Jr. *Prevailing Wage Legislation: The Davis-Bacon Act, State "Little Davis-Bacon" Acts, The Walsh-Healey Act, and The Service Contract Act*. Philadelphia, the Wharton School, University of Pennsylvania, 1986. p. 93-94.
[7] Thieblot, *The Davis-Bacon Act*, p. 170.
[8] Allen, Steven G., and David Reich. *Prevailing Wage Laws Are Not Inflationary: A Case Study of Public School Construction Costs*. Washington, Center to Protect Workers' Rights, December 1980. p. iii.

Department, AFL-CIO. Allen has developed this theme in subsequent academic work and is often cited.

A 1982 study, *Effect of the Davis-Bacon Act on Construction Costs in Non-Metropolitan Areas of the United States*, was prepared by Martha N. Frauyndorf (with others) of Oregon State University. Raundorf suggests that the cost estimates for Davis-Bacon offered by GAO, Thieblot, and certain others are based on "an erroneous procedure" and she chides GAO for working from a sample even the agency recognized was "really too small for extrapolation."[9] But, the Oregon team, funded by the American Farm Bureau Federation (a critic of Davis-Bacon), was forced to scale back its own work because of difficulties it encountered in securing adequate data.

Fraundorf and her colleagues began with an assumption: "While it is fairly clear that the law results in higher wages, it does not follow that the law therefore raises overall costs." To determine the latter, they attempted an empirical study of total costs. But, they found this to be complex. First, they looked only at rural non-residential construction – which, they conceded, might differ from urban work. Second, they could not disaggregate Davis-Bacon costs from other federal requirements: i.e., "affirmative action, or different standards for quality and safety." Third, they were not able to access varying "alternative method[s] of construction." Within those parameters, they compared federal with non-federal construction, concluding: "While the exact size of the impact is still uncertain, our results show that it is likely to be between 26% and 38%."[10]

Frequently cited in the Davis-Bacon literature is the work of economists Robert Goldfarb and John Morrall. Begun as public research for the U.S. Council on Wage and Price Stability (COWPS) during the mid-1970s, the work of Goldfarb and Morrall was further developed in a series of private academic articles. At COWPS, they found themselves working with data provided by DOL which they viewed as not entirely satisfactory for this purposes. In their COWPS analysis (1976), they identified the deficiencies they found in the data they were using and spoke of "some rough order of magnitude" of "possible cost savings" from changes in the administration of

---

[9] Fraundorf, Martha Norby, with John P. Farrell, and Robert Mason. *Effect of the Davis-Bacon Act on Construction Costs in Non-Metropolitan Areas of the United States.* Corvallis, The Oregon State University, 1972. p. 4-5. (Hereafter cited as Fraundorf, *et al., Effect of the Davis-Bacon Act on Construction Costs.*)

[10] Fraundorf, *et al., Effect of the Davis-Bacon Act on Construction Costs*, p. 27. The authors note: "Furthermore, if the Davis-Bacon Act were repealed, it would not mean a 26.1% decrease in costs unless state prevailing wage laws (which would still apply to many, but not all, projects) also were repealed."

Davis-Bacon. But, they cautioned by way of conclusion: "... the data are somewhat ambiguous and perhaps unreliable."[11]

In a private academic article (1978), Goldfarb and Morrall seem to have been somewhat less cautious suggesting that, with administrative changes with respect to Davis-Bacon, "an overall savings in the hundreds of millions is possible." And, they point out, various administrative changes "might well encourage an expansion of the nonunion sector, which might in turn have cost-lowering effects in the long run."[12]

Their work sparked some criticism which, in yet another article (1981), they attempted to refute. Critiques, in the abstract, are difficult to evaluate and, even more so, critiques of critiques; and, by the early 1980s, the literature was beset by argument and counter argument, often focusing (as Goldfarb and Morrall had done themselves in 1976) upon the inadequacies of the data. Seeming to share the approach of Thieblot (and, like Thieblot, basing their work on pre-Reagan data), Goldfarb and Morrall acknowledge the data problems but reject the notion "that this invalidates the usefulness of cost calculations." They affirm, rather, that even "rough estimates of possible magnitudes of effects based on imperfect data are very useful background information for helping inform policy decisions."[13]

During the early 1980s, a private sector body working under the auspices of the Reagan Administration reviewed the operation of the federal government and recommended ways in which to effect efficiency and reduce costs. The Grace Commission, as it was popularly known, examined the operation of the Davis-Bacon Act (among other statutes and programs). Its review of Davis-Bacon, frequently cited at the time, was based on prior studies rather than original research. Thus, it was subject to all of the strengths and weaknesses of the earlier research upon which it relied.[14]

---

[11] Goldfarb, Robert S., and John F. Morrall. *An Analysis of Certain Aspects of the Administration of the Davis-Bacon Act.* Washington, Council on Wage and Price Stability, May 1976. p. 3 and 14.

[12] Goldfarb, Robert S., and John F. Morrall. Cost Implications of Changing Davis-Bacon Administration. *Policy Analysis,* fall 1978. p. 449-451.

[13] Goldfarb, Robert S., and John F. Morrall. The Davis-Bacon Act: an Appraisal of Recent Studies. *Industrial and Labor Relations Review,* January 1981. p. 200.

[14] Concerning the Grace Commission and its work, see: *DLR,* November 10, 1983, p. A2-A5; Cohen, Robert M. Reagan's Cost Control 'Bloodhounds' Are Hounded by Charges of Conflicts. *National Journal,* January 15, 1983. p. 122-124; Hayes, Robert M. The President's Private Sector Survey on Cost Control: An Opinion Essay on the Grace Commission Report. *Government Information Quarterly,* v. 3, no. 1, 1986. p. 73-81; and, Grace, J. Peter. The President's Private Sector Survey on Cost Control: A Response to an Opinion Essay on Its Proposals. *Government Information Quarterly,* v. 3, no. 2, 1986. p. 153-161.

In 1985, Chairman J. Peter Grace reviewed the work of the commission in testimony before the Senate Committee on Governmental Affairs. Evidencing some exasperation with quibbles over impact estimates in general, he urged that policymakers should set aside the dispute about "how accurate the numbers are" and get on with the business of reform. "No one can ever tell what something will save until one does it," he affirmed.[15] While many may share Grace's frustration, others may argue that numbers *do* matter and that reasonable precision is important – especially when cost-savings projections become a central rationale in public policy formation.

During recent years, Peter Philips, professor of economics at the University of Utah, with others, has produced a number of analyses of the impact of state "little Davis-Bacon" acts or of the repeal of such statutes. Speaking generally, these studies appear to have found a certain utility in prevailing wage legislation: i.e., that prevailing wage statutes may (and, likely do) have positive economic impacts for the community apart from any advantage to workers. Further, they seem to suggest that allegations of negative impact (for example, unjustifiably inflating the cost of public construction – or increasing such costs at all) may be overstated.[16]

---

[15] U.S. Congress. Senate. Committee on Governmental Affairs. *Oversight of the Implementation of the Grace Commission Report.* Hearing. 99th Cong., 1st Sess. May 9, 1985. Washington, U.S. Govt. Print. Off., 1985. p. 109. Chairman Grace's affirmation to the Committee notwithstanding, he had asserted in his book, *Burning Money: The Waste of Your Tax Dollars* (New York, Macmillan, 1984), p. 175: "Repeal of the [Davis-Bacon] Act would save the Government $4.97 billion over three years."

[16] Philips, Peter, Garth Mangum, Norm Waitzman, and Anne Yeagle. *Losing Ground: A Report on the Repeal of Nine Little Davis-Bacon Acts.* Salt Lake City, University of Utah Press, 1995. 83 p.; Philips, Hamid Azari-Rad, and Anne Yeagle. The Effects of the Repeal of Utah's Prevailing Wage Law on the Labor Market in Construction (in Friedman, Sheldon, et al., editors), *Restoring the Promise of American Labor Law.* Ithaca, Cornell University Press, 1994. p. 207-222; and Philips, Peter. *Square Foot Construction Costs for Newly Constructed State and Local Schools, Offices and Warehouses in Nine Southwestern and Intermountain States, 1992-1994.* Prepared for the Legislative Education Study Committee of the New Mexico State Legislature. September 6, 1996. 43 p.

BIBLIOGRAPHY

Through the years, the Davis-Bacon Act has attracted considerable attention from economists, attorneys, policy analysts, journalists and others. The result is a moderately extensive bibliography of materials readily available to the public. Its quality, as noted above, varies from one item to another.

Most of the entries in this bibliography deal specifically with Davis-Bacon. There are, however, a number that focus upon issues related tangentially (but importantly) to questions that have been raised about the application of the Act. For example, an extensive literature has been developed dealing with the impact of trade unions upon productivity, a central factor in estimating the cost impact of the Act. A representative sample of these studies has been included in the listing. Also included are a number of entries bearing upon the nature of the construction industry and upon legal issues associated with administration of the Davis-Bacon Act and with its impact.

This bibliography is selective. While primarily of published materials, it also includes, in a few instances, materials that have not been published but which have been widely circulated through the years and/or which have had an impact upon the Davis-Bacon debate. Because its focus is primarily upon analytical or policy literature, a listing of congressional hearings and reports has not been included – thought these have been cited in the footnotes of the covering essay as appropriate. Also omitted (with select exceptions) are studies produced by the Department of Labor and the several legislative branch agencies such as the General Accounting Office and the Congressional Budget Office.

There has been, through the years, a significant reportage concerning the Davis-Bacon Act in the industry and trade union press; sometimes brief editorial comment; on other occasions, publication of testimony presented before a committee of the Congress or an analysis of legislation. For the most part, these industry and trade union materials have not been included – though this latter policy has not been followed uniformly. Finally, there are a number of manuals – how to administer the Act, how to conduct wage surveys, how to comply with the provisions of the statute – that have been prepared by an agency or one of the interest groups. These, too, have been omitted from the listing here.

For the most part, items listed in the bibliography are available from the general collection of the Library of Congress and, frequently, are also available from university collections and public libraries.

Addison, John T. Are unions good for productivity? Journal of labor research, spring 1982: 125-138.
-------. and John B. Chilton. Can we identify union productivity effects? Industrial relations, winter 1993: 124-132.
Addison, John T., and Barry T. Hirsch. The Economic Analysis of Unions: New Approaches and Evidence. Boston, Allen & Unwin, 1986. [See Chapter 9, "Unions and Politics," p. 268-295.]
Alario, Linda E. Project Agreements and Government Procurement. Industrial and Labor Relations Review, October 1996: 17-30.
Allen, Steven G. Can Union Labor Ever Cost Less? The Quarterly Journal of Economics, May 1987: 347-373.
-------. Developments in Collective Bargaining in Construction in the 1980s and 1990s. Cambridge, National Bureau of Economic Research, Inc., working paper no. 4674, March 1994. 40 p.
-------. Declining Unionization in Construction: The Facts and the Reasons. Industrial and Labor Relations Review, April 1988: 343-359.
-------. Declining Unionization in Construction: Fresh Facts and New Reasons. Workplace Topics, June 1994: 45-60.
-------. Further Evidence on Union Efficiency in Construction. Industrial Relations, spring 1988: 232-240.
-------. Human Resource Policies and Union-Nonunion Productivity Differences. Cambridge, National Bureau of Economic Research, Inc., working paper no. 2744, October 1988. 39 p.
-------. Much Ado About Davis-Bacon: A Critical Review and New Evidence. Journal of Law and Economics, October 1983: 707-736.

--------. Productivity Levels and Productivity Change Under Unionism. Industrial Relations, winter 1988: 94-112.

--------. Union Work Rules and Efficiency in the Building Trades. Journal of Labor Economics, April 1986: 212-242.

--------. Unionization and Productivity in Office Building and School Construction. Cambridge, National Bureau of Economic Research, Inc., working paper no. 1139, June 1983. 46 p.

--------. Unionization and Productivity in Office Building and School Construction. Industrial and Labor Relations Review, January 1986: 187-201.

--------. Unionized Construction Workers are More Productive. Washington, Center to Protect Workers' Rights, November 1979. 25 p.

--------. Unions and Efficiency in Private Sector Construction: Further Evidence. Cambridge, National Bureau of Economic Research, working paper no. 2254. May 1987. 23 p.

--------. Unit Costs, Legal Shocks, and Unionization in Construction. Journal of Labor Research, summer 1995: 367-385.

--------. Why Construction Industry Productivity is Declining. Review of Economics and Statistics, November 1985: 661-669.

--------, and David Reich. Prevailing Wage Laws are Not Inflationary: A Case Study of Public School Construction Costs. Washington, Center to Protect Workers' Rights, December 1980. 24 p.

Barrow, Clyde W. Unions and Community Mobilization: The 1988 Massachusetts prevailing Wage Campaign. Labor Studies Journal, winter 1989: 18-39.

Barry, Patrick. Congress's Deconstruction Theory. Washington Monthly, January 1990: 10-14, 16.

Beard, Edward P. Straight Talk about Davis-Bacon: An Interview with Representative Edward P. Beard, D-RI. Builders, v. 1, April 9, 1979: 1-4.

Berg, John T., and Ralph C. Erickson. An Evaluation of the Impact of the Davis-Bacon Act. Government Union Review, summer 1975: 1-32.

Bernstein, David.Bring Jim Crow to an End by Repealing the Davis-Bacon Act. USA Today [Magazine]. July 1993: 14-16.

--------. Clinton Should Scrap Davis-Bacon. Human Events, March 6, 1993: 11.

--------. The Davis-Bacon Act: Let's Bring Jim Crow to an End. The Cato Institute, Briefing Paper No. 17, January 18, 1993. 15 p.

[See also, The David-Bacon Act: A Response to the CATO Institute's Attack. Washington, Building and Construction Trades Department, AFL-CIO, 1993. 26 p.]

――――. The Davis-Bacon Act: Vestige of Jim Crow. National Black Law Journal, fall 1994: 276-297.

――――. Exclusionary Rule: Something's Not Kosher about Davis-Bacon. Reason, August/September 1991: 32-35.

――――. It's Time to Reform New York's Prevailing Wage Law. Empire Foundation for Public Policy Research, September 1993. [Published in updated form in the George Mason Civil Rights Law Journal, spring 1997. See next entry.]

――――. The Shameful, Wasteful History of New York's Prevailing Wage Law. George Mason University Civil Rights Law Journal, spring 1997: 1-23.

――――. The Supreme Court and "Civil Rights," 1886-1908. The Yale Law Journal, December 1990: 725-744.

――――. Roots of the 'underclass': The Decline of Laissez-Faire Jurisprudence and the Rise of Racist Labor Legislation. The American University Law Review, fall 1993: 85-138.

Bolick, Clint. The Revolt Against the Davis-Bacon Act. The American Enterprise, january/February 1997: 78-79.

Bourdon, Clinton C., and Raymond E. Levitt. Cost Impacts of Prevailing Wage Laws in Construction. Journal of the Construction Division, American Society of Civil Engineers, December 1979: 281-288.

――――. The Impact of the Davis-Bacon Act. In: Union and Open-shop Construction. Lexington, Massachusetts, Lexington Books, 1980. p. 91-103.

――――, and Arthur P. Solomon. The Inflationary Effects of the Davis-Bacon Act: A Summary and Analysis of the Research Literature. Report prepared for the U.S. Department of Housing and Urban Development, July 2, 1979. 37 p. (Mimeographed)

Brazier, Nona. The Devils of Davis-Bacon. Common Sense, fall 1994: 24-34.

Brown, Charles, and James Medoff. Trade Unions in the Production process. Journal of Political Economy, June 1978: 355-378.

Brown, William W. The Challenges of a Changing Workforce. Constructor, April 1992: 23-26.

Brozen, Yale. The Davis-Bacon Act: How to Load the Dice Against Yourself. Manuscript, in mimeograph form, in the files of the Congressional Research Service, 1971. 9 p.

-------. The Law That Boomeranged. Nation's Business, April 1974: 70-73.
Buchsbaum, Pater A., and Mark Erlich. The Debate Over Union Wage Requirements for Subsidized Housing. Shelter Force, March/April 1993: 12-14.
Burck, Gilbert. A Time of Reckoning for the Building Unions. Fortune, June 4, 1979: 82-85, 88, 93-94, and 96.
-------. The Building Trades Versus the People. Fortune. October 1970: 94-97, and 159-160.
Caruso, Lawrence R. An analysis of the litigation regarding the regulations implementing the Davis-Bacon Act. Federal bar news & journal, March 1984: 117-122.
Chin, Felix. The Davis-Bacon Act: a selected bibliography. Monticello, Ill., Vance bibliographies, 1981. 22 p.
Clark, Kim B. The impact of unionization on productivity: a case study. Industrial and labor relations review, July 1980: 451-469.
Cox, Louis A. The Davis-Bacon Act and defense construction: problems of statutory coverage. In Stein, Manual, ed., Proceedings of the fifteenth annual New York University conference on labor, June 11-13, 1962. New York, Matthew Bender & company, inc., 1962: 151-174.
DeLury, Bernard E. Davis-Bacon: an insider's viewpoint. The international operating engineer, December 1975: 10-11.
Derthick, Martha, and Paul J. Quirk. The politics of deregulation. Washington, The Brookings Institution, 1985. p. 219-224.
Dillon, Rodger. Potential economic impact: Proposals of the Department of Industrial Relations to alter methodology relating to prevailing wages. Sacramento, California Senate office of Research. Stock number 862-S, May 1996. 28 p.
Donahue, Charles. The Davis-Bacon Act and the Walsh-Healey public contracts act: a comparison of coverage and minimum wage provisions. Law and contemporary problems, spring 1964: 488-513.
Easterbrook, Greg. How big labor brings home the bacon. The Washington monthly, February 1991: 40-47.
Eberly, Don. Labor as a property right: guaranteeing economic opportunity. Lincoln review, spring 1983: 31-47.
Elisburg, Donald. Wage protection under the Davis-Bacon Act. Labor law journal, June 1977: 323-328.
Erlick, Mark. Labor at the ballot box: The Massachusetts prevailing wage campaign of 1988. Philadelphia, Temple University Press, 1990. 219 p.

-------. Labor rises up to show the way. The Nation, December 26, 1988: 716-718.

-------. Who will build the future? Labor research review, Fall 1988: 1-19.

Fine, Janice. Organizing for prevailing wage in Florida. labor research review, Fall 1988: 71-79.

Fine, Sidney. "Without Blare of Trumpets" – Walter Drew, the National Erector's Association, and the open shop movement, 1903-57. Ann Arbor, The University of Michigan Press, 1995. 384 p.

Foster, Howard G. Industrial relations in construction, 1970-1977. Industrial relations, February 1978: 1-17.

-------. Manpower in homebuilding: a preliminary analysis. Philadelphia, The Wharton School, University of Pennsylvania, 1974. 179 p.

-------. The labor market in nonunion construction. Industrial and labor relations review, July 1973: 1071-1085.

-------, and Herbert Northrup. Open shop construction. Philadelphia, The Wharton School, University of Pennsylvania, 1975. 394 p.

-------, and George Strauss. Labor problems in construction: a review. Industrial relations, October 1972: 289-313.

Fowler, George. Davis-Bacon needs a decent burial. Nation's business, March 1979: 57-60.

Foxvog, Donald R. Industry's united position: On missile base sites, 'construction work by construction men.' The constructor, July 1960: 45-46, 49-51.

Franklin, William S. A comparison of formally and informally trained journeymen in construction. Industrial and labor relations review, July 1973: 1086-1094.

Fraundorf, Martha Norby, with John P. Farrell and Robert Mason. Effect of the Davis-Bacon Act on construction costs in non-metropolitan areas of the United States. Corvallis, The Oregon State University, January 1982. 41 p.

-------. The effect of the Davis-Bacon Act on construction costs in rural areas. The review of economics and statistics, February 1984: 142-146.

Freeman, Richard B. and James L. Medoff. The two faces of unionism. The public interest, fall 1979: 69-93.

Funk, William G. The Paperwork Reduction Act: Paperwork reduction meets administrative law. Harvard journal on legislation, winter 1987: 1-116.

Gallaway, Lowell, and Richard Vedder. Cracked foundation: repealing the Davis-Bacon Act. St. Louis, Washington University Center for the

Study of American Business. Policy study number 127, November 1995. 28 p.

-------. Labor laws: then and now. Journal of labor research, spring 1996: 253-275.

-------. Out of work: unemployment and government in twentieth-century America. New York, Holmes & Meier, 1993.

-------. Why Johnny can't work: the cause of unemployment. Policy review, fall 1992: 24-30.

Goldfarb, Robert S. A Davis-Bacon musicale: symphony orchestras as migrant labor. Journal of labor research, fall 1984: 427-433.

-------, and Michael R. Metzger. Do Davis-Bacon minimum wages raise product quality? Journal of labor research, summer 1983: 265-272.

-------, and John F. Morall. An analysis of certain aspects of the administration of the Davis-Bacon Act. Washington, The Council on Wage and Price Stability, 1976. 14 p. (Mimeographed)

-------. Cost implications of changing Davis-Bacon administration. Policy analysis, fall 1978: 439-453.

-------. The Davis-Bacon Act: an appraisal of recent studies. Industrial and labor relations review, January 1981: 191-206.

Goldfinger, Nathaniel. The myth of housing costs. American federationist, December 1969: 1-6.

Gould, John P. Davis-Bacon Act: the economics of prevailing wage laws. Washington, The American enterprise institute, November 1971. 44 p.

-------. The labor component in the cost of housing. In: Housing in the seventies: working papers, I. Washington, U.S. Govt. Print. Off., 1976. p. 588-597.

-------, and George Bittlingmayer. The economics of the Davis-Bacon Act: an analysis of prevailing wage laws. Washington, The American enterprise institute, 1980. 89 p.

Gramm, Phil. The inapplicability of the Davis-Bacon Act to military construction projects. Labor law journal, July 1985: 387-389.

Gujarati, D.N. The economics of the Davis-Bacon Act. Journal of business, July 1967: 303-316.

Haber, William. Industrial relations in the building industry. Cambridge, Harvard University Press, 1930. 578 p.

-------, and Harold Levinson. Labor relations and productivity in the building trades. Ann Arbor, University of Michigan, 1956. 260 p.

Hartman, Paul T. and Walter H. Franke. The changing bargaining structure in construction: wide-area and multicraft bargaining. Industrial and labor relations review, January 1980: 170-184.

Hermanson, Beth. Pennsylvania's prevailing wage act: an appropriate target for ERISA preemption. Dickinson law review, summer 1996: 919-962.

Hill, Norman. Minorities, women and the Davis-Bacon Act: The most vulnerable. National journal, September 19, 1981: 1700-1701.

Hintze, Arthur. Taking the waste out of Davis-Bacon. Constructor, June 1977: 16-17, and 43.

--------. A Davis-Bacon Primer. Constructor, June 1975: 15-16, 33.

--------. Can Davis-Bacon decisions be reviewed? Constructor, January 1967: 51-52.

--------. How to comply with Davis-Bacon rules. Constructor, November 1975: 34-36.

--------. Unscrambling Davis-Bacon administration. Constructor, August 1975: 34-36.

Hoehn, James G. The Davis-Bacon Act: an example of the problems of wage-price administration. Economic review, published by the Federal Reserve Bank of Dallas, March 1982: 13-18.

Hunter, William J. Discriminatory effects of Wisconsin's prevailing wage laws. Milwaukee, A heartland policy study, December 2, 1988. 17 p.

In search of a cure for Davis-Bacon. Nation's business, July 1981: 60-62.

Isokait, William A. Anatomy of a victory: reason restored, courts rule Davis-Bacon Act language means what it says. Constructor, August 1994: 20-22.

--------. Davis-Bacon developments after *Midway Excavators*. Constructor, July 1991: 100-102.

--------. Project labor agreements: an industry perspective. Journal of labor research, Winter 1998: 65-71.

--------. Reason restored: courts rule Davis-Bacon Act language means what it says. Constructor, August 1994: 20-22.

--------. What *Midway Excavators* means for federal construction contractors. Constructor, August 1992: 27-29.

Jenkins, Kirk. Congress: Waging war over the prevailing wage. Harvard political review, Spring 1982: 16.

Johnson, David B. Prevailing wage law. In Somers, Gerald G., ed. Labor, management, and social policy: essays in the John R. Commons tradition. Madison, The University of Wisconsin Press, 1963. p. 231-262.

------. Prevailing wage legislation in the states. Monthly labor review, August 1961: 839-845.

Kentucky. General Assembly. Legislative Research Commission. Capital Construction and Equipment Purchase Oversight Committee. The economic impact of the Kentucky prevailing wage law. Frankfort, 1981. 129 p. (Research report no. 185)

Kessler, Daniel P., and Lawrence F. Katz. Prevailing wage laws and construction labor markets. Industrial and labor relations review, January 2001: 259-274. [An earlier version of this article appeared as National Bureau of Economic Research Working Paper No. W7454. December 1999.]

Keyes, William A. The minimum wage and the Davis-Bacon Act: employment effects on minorities and youth. Journal of labor research, fall 1982: 399-413.

------. Why the Davis-Bacon Act means unemployment. Lincoln review, autumn 1979: 29-38.

Kovach, Kenneth A. Should the Davis-Bacon Act be repealed? Business horizons, September-October 1983: 33-37.

------, and Laura Viehmyer Eide. The case for repeal of the Davis-Bacon Act. Labor law journal, January 1998: 761-772.

Lanouette, William L. Foes may use salami tactics to wipe the Davis-Bacon Act off the books. National journal, September 5, 1981: 1587-1591.

Leader, Laurie E., and Kenneth A. Jenero. Implied private right of action under the Davis-Bacon Act: closing some loopholes in administrative enforcement. DePaul law review, Spring 1980: 793-817.

Lee, Gene Ming. A case for fairness in public works contracting. Fordham law review, December 1996: 1075-1121. [The focus of the article is upon the nature of public works contracting, not the Davis-Bacon Act specifically.]

Levinson, David. The hard-hats, the Davis-Bacon Act and Nixon's incomes policy. Labor law journal, June 1971: 323-331.

Levitt, Raymond E. Union versus nonunion construction in the U.S. Journal of the construction division, American society of civil engineers, December 1979: 289-303.

Lindauer, Stephen R. Use of subjourneymen: a competitive advantage. Constructor, May 1985: 79-80.

Lindsey, Lawrence B. Increased opportunity through deregulation. Government union review, Fall 1994: 43-51.

Lyons, Max. The estimated cost of project labor agreements on federal construction, Journal of labor research, Winter 1998: 73-87.

Mainland, Mary. 'Prevailing' wages. America, February 22, 1986: 140-142.

Mandelstamm, Allan B. The effects of unions on efficiency in the residential construction industry: a case study. Industrial and labor relations review, July 1965: 503-521.

Marshall, Ray. America still needs Davis-Bacon. National journal, October 10, 1981: 1837-1939.

Martin, Christopher J., and John F. Meyers. Court rejects efforts to impose prevailing wages on private sector employers. Employee relations law journal, v. 17, no. 3, winter 1991-1992: 483-489.

Martucci, William C., and John L. Utz. Special construction industry provisions under the multiemployer pension plan amendments act. Labor law journal, May 1984: 281-288.

McAllister, Eugene J. Davis-Bacon: a costly contradiction. Backgrounder no. 88. Washington, the Heritage foundation, June 14, 1979. 11 p.

Melman, Stephen J. Davis-Bacon prevails. Housing economics, May 1994: 9-10.

Methvin, Eugene H. A scandalous law that's costing taxpayers billions. Reader's digest, December 1994: 123-126.

Mills, D. Quinn. Explaining pay increases in construction: 1953-1972. Industrial relations, May 1974: 196-201.

-------. Industrial relations and manpower in construction. Cambridge, the Massachusetts institute of technology press, 1972. 297 p.

Miller, Scott. Preemptive effect of ERISA on the prevailing wage act. The John Marshall law review, fall 1995: 55-73.

Mitchell, Merwin W., and Joe A. Stone. Union effects on productivity: evidence from western U.S. sawmills. Industrial and labor relations review, October 1992: 135-145.

Morowitz, Lisa. Government contracts, social legislation, and prevailing wages: enforcing the Davis-Bacon Act. In the public interest [Amherst, New York], spring 1989: 29-42.

Muller, Thomas, and Michael Fix. Federal solicitude, local costs: the impact of federal regulation on municipal finances. Regulations: AEI journal on government and society, July/August 1980: 29-36.

Murchison, Kenneth M. Local government law. Louisiana law review, January 1993: 823-861. [Pages 841-848 focus upon Louisiana's prevailing wage statute.]

Murphy, Cait. Unfinished business: who's holding up Grace Commission reform? Policy Review, fall 1986: 60-65.

Northrup, Herbert R. The 'helper' controversy in the construction industry. Journal of labor research, fall 1992: 421-435.

-------. Construction union programs to regain jobs: background and overview. Journal of labor research, winter 1997: 1-15.

-------, and Linda E. Alario. "Boston Harbor"-type project labor agreements in construction: nature, rationales, and legal challenges. Journal of labor research, Winter 1998: 1-63.

-------, and Augustus White. Subsidizing contractors to gain employment: construction union 'job targeting.' Berkeley journal of employment and labor law, no. 1, 1966: 62-90.

O'Connell, John F. The effects of Davis-Bacon on labor cost and union wages. Journal of labor research, summer 1986: 239-253.

Payne, Phillis. The plot to subvert labor standards. American federationist, July 1979: 17-21.

Pendolino, Timothy J. The Davis-Bacon and Service Contracts Acts: laws whose time has passed? Military law review, winter 1995: 218-261.

Philips, Peter. Square foot construction costs for newly constructed state and local schools, offices and warehouses in nine southwestern and intermountain states, 1992-1994. Prepared for the Legislative Education Study Committee of the New Mexico State Legislature. Salt Lake City, September 6, 1996. 43 p.

-------, Hamid Azari-Rad, and Anne Yeagle. The effects of the repeal of Utah's prevailing wage law on the labor market in construction. In Friedman, Sheldon, et al., editors, Restoring the promise of American labor law. Ithaca, Cornell University Press, 1994: 207-222.

-------, Garth Mangum, Norm Waitzman, and Yeagle. Losing ground: a report on the repeal of nine little Davis-Bacon Acts. Salt Lake City, University of Utah Press, 1995. 83 p.

Pohlman, Jerry E. Hard-core unemployment, public housing construction and the Davis-Bacon Act. Labor law journal, April 1971: 195-203.

President's private sector survey on cost control. Report on the department of labor. Approved by the subcommittee for the full executive committee, spring-fall 1983. [Washington] President's private sector survey on cost control, 1983. 91-102.

Price, W. S. A review of the application of the Davis-Bacon Act. Labor law journal, July 1963: 614-636.

Raphaelson, Arnold H. The Davis-Bacon Act. In, Zeckhauser, Richard J., and Derek Leebaert (eds.). What role for government? Lessons from policy research. Durham, Duke Press Policy Studies, 1983. 123-136, 336-337.

Reich, Michael. Prevailing wage laws and the California economy. Berkeley, institute of industrial relations, February 1996. 18 p. [Unpublished paper.]

Reynolds, Morgan O. Making America poorer: the cost of labor law. Washington, the Cato institute, 1987. 210 p.

--------. Power and privilege: labor unions in America. New York, Universe books, 1984. 301 p.

--------. Trade unions in the production process. Journal of political economy, April 1986: 443-447.

--------. Understanding political pricing of labor services: the Davis-Bacon Act. Journal of labor research, summer 1982: 295-309.

Roberts, James H. Falsification of certified payrolls: the 'smoking pistol' of Davis-Bacon Act debarment. General accounting office, office of the general counsel. OGC adviser, v. 3, Jan. 1979: 9-11.

Roberts, Kenneth M. The Davis-Bacon Act, another setback for labor: *Building & Construction Trades Department v. Donovan.* The journal of corporate law, fall 1984: 277-290.

Ross, Irwin. The outdated law that's costing taxpayers billions. The reader's digest, December 1981: 43-48.

Reducing the federal budget: strategies and examples. A background paper. Congressional budget office. Washington, February 1980. 68 p.

Rowan, Richard L., and Lester Rubin. Opening the skilled construction trades to blacks: a study of the Washington and Indianapolis plans for minority employment. Philadelphia, the Wharton School, University of Pennsylvania, 1972. 193 p.

Rothman, Stuart. The work of the wage appeals board with respect to the Davis-Bacon and related federal construction laws. Constructor, September 1964: 34-37.

Sautter, Udo. Government and unemployment: The use of public works before the New Deal. Journal of American history, June 1986: 59-86.

Scheibla, Shirley Hobbs. Big labor's big rip-off. Conservative digest. February 1979: 14-16.

--------. Powerful lever: how the Davis-Bacon Act jacks up construction costs. Barron's, August 28, 1978: 4-6.

Schooner, Steven L. The Davis-Bacon Act: controversial implementation of the 50 percent rule. Employee relations law journal, spring 1985: 702-716.

Schulman, Stuart. The case against the Davis-Bacon Act. Government union review, winter 1983: 23-39.

Schumer, Fern. Fighting words in Washington. Forbes, May 14, 1979: 92-93.

Seligman, Daniel. How to pay a painter. Fortune, July 30, 1990: 258-260.

Singer, James W. Bringing home the Davis-Bacon. National journal, March 31, 1979: 531.

--------. Who will prevail on the prevailing wage laws? National journal, January 27, 1979: 140-144.

Speck, William H. The liability of the United States upon wage schedules in construction contracts. The George Washington law review, January 1955: 249-283.

Stevenson, Charles. Your move on inflation, Mr. President. The reader's digest. April 1975: 157-162.

Stone, Joseph M., and John R. Brunozzi. The construction worker under federal wage laws. Washington, The Livingston press, 1959. 129 p.

The Davis-Bacon Act: it works to build America. Washington, The building and construction trades department, AFL-CIO, September 1979. 82 p.

The GAO on Davis-Bacon: a fatally flawed study. Washington, Center to protect workers' rights, September 1978. 18 p.

The 1990 West Virginia prevailing wage law study. University of West Virginia, College of Graduate Studies, School of Business and Management, summer 1990: 33-45.

Thieblot, Armand J., Jr. A new evaluation of impacts of prevailing wage law repeal. Journal of labor research, spring 1996: 297-322.

--------. Fraud prevalent in prevailing wage surveys. Government union review, Spring 1998: 1-30.

--------. Prevailing wage laws and black employment in the construction industry. Journal of labor research, Winter 1999: 155-159.

--------. Prevailing wage laws and market recovery strategies of construction unions. Journal of labor research, Winter 1997: 31-46.

--------. Prevailing wage laws and school construction costs. Washington, The merit shop foundation, n.d. 16 p.

--------. Prevailing wage laws of the states. Government union review, fall 1983: 3-65.

--------. Prevailing wage laws of the states and the District of Columbia: a review compendium. Washington, The merit shop foundation, September 1980. 43 p.

--------. Prevailing wage legislation: the Davis-Bacon Act, state "little Davis-Bacon" acts, the Walsh-Healey Act, and the Service Contract Act. Philadelphia, The Wharton school, university of Pennsylvania, 1986. 273 p.

--------. State prevailing wage laws: an assessment at the start of 1995. Rosslyn, Va., State Relations Department, Associated Builders and Contractors, 1995: 1-39.

--------. The "little Davis-Bacon Acts" – prevailing wage laws of the states. Washington, The merit shop foundation, August 1976. 39 p.

--------. The Davis-Bacon Act. Philadelphia, The Wharton school, university of Pennsylvania, 1975. 233 p.

Turnbull, Peter J. Trade unions and productivity: opening the Harvard 'black boxes'. Journal of labor research, spring 1991: 135-150.

Tyson, William S. Prevailing wage determinations in the construction industry: some legal aspects. Labor law journal, November 1952: 776-788.

U.S. Congressional Budget Office. Modifying the Davis-Bacon Act: implications for the labor market and the federal budget. [Prepared by Steven H. Sheingold.] Washington, U.S. Govt. Print. Off., July 1983. 49 p.

U.S. General Accounting Office. The Davis-Bacon Act should be repealed. Report by the Comptroller General of the United States. Washington, U.S. Govt. Print. Off., April 22, 1979, 276 p.

Van Dam, Laura. Will prevailing wage prevail over attack by business groups? High costs under fire. New England business, November 4, 1985: 45-46.

Van de Water, John R. Applications of labor law to construction and equipping of United States missile bases. Labor law journal, November 1961: 1003-1024.

Vincent, Jeff. Indiana's prevailing wage law: a preliminary evaluation of its impact on the state construction industry. Labor studies journal, fall 1990: 17-31.

Walsh, Edward J. White paper: organized labor ... the Davis-Bacon Act. Government union review, fall 1985: 25-28.

Warner, John W. Congressional and administrative efforts to modify or eliminate the Davis-Bacon Act. Western state university law review, fall 1982: 1-22.

Welch, Stephen W. Union-nonunion construction wage differentials. Industrial relations, spring 1980: 152-162.

# Bibliography

Wells, Robert Marshall. GOP planning to topple wall of rules around workplace. Congressional quarterly, May 13, 1995: 1328-1330.
Wolk, Stuart Rodney. Davis-Bacon: labor's anachronism, 1974. Labor law journal, July 1974: 404-407.
-------. Mr. Davis-Mr. Bacon – but who is the enforcer? Labor law journal, June 1964: 323-326.
-------. The case of confused application. Labor law journal, November 1966: 694-697.
-------. The fringe benefit amendment to the Davis-Bacon Act. Labor law journal, October 1964: 673-677.
Wyckoff, Viola. The public works wage rate and some of its economic effects. New York, Columbia university press, 1946. 307 p.
Zanglein, Jayne Elizabeth. To preempt or not to preempt: will the Supreme Court do some serious bushhogging through the preemption thicket? Journal of pension planning and compliance, Fall 1997: 22-38.

INDEX

A

academic studies, 16
academic work, 16, 20
administrative personnel, 16
affirmative action, 20
Allen, Steven, 19
anti-kickback, vii, 4

B

Bacon, Representative Robert L., 2
better workmanship, 12
bidding, 3
broadly skilled, 11
building trades, 12, 29
Bush Administration, 9
Bush, President George, vii, 9

C

Carter Administration, 7, 8
Center to Protect Workers' Rights, 19, 25
certified program, 12
Clinton, President William, 10
competition, 11, 12

Congress, iii, 1, 3-, 12, 17, 18, 22, 24, 25, 30
Congressional Budget Office(CBO), 17-19, 23, 36
congressional hearings, 8, 15, 23
constitutional authority, 1
construction contracts, ix, 35
construction field, 2
Construction Industry Stabilization Committee, 7
construction industry, 7, 9, 12, 23, 32, 33, 35, 36
construction work, ix, 28
contracting out, 2
contractors, vii, 2, 3, 5, 11, 12, 16, 30, 33
Copeland "Anti-Kickback" Act, 4, 9
Copeland Act, 9, 12, 16
Copeland, Senator Royal, 4
Council on Wage and Price Stability (COWPS), 20

D

Davis, Senator James, 2
Davis-Bacon Amendments, 5
Department of Labor (DOL), 6-8, 17, 20, 23
District of Columbia, 5, 35

documentation, 16, 17
Donovan, Raymond, 8

E

economic impact, 16, 27, 31

F

Fair Labor Standards Act, 1, 12
federal construction work, 2, 12
federal contracting practice, 2
federal contracting procedures, 11
federal government, ix, 1, 15, 21
federal program statutes, vii
federal projects, 3
federally financed construction, 4
"fly-by-night" firms, 12
Ford Administration, 7
Frauyndorf, Martha N., 20
fringe benefit, vii, ix, 6, 37

G

General Accounting Office (GAO), 6, 8, 17, 18, 20, 23, 35, 36
general utility workers, 11
Goldfarb, Robert, 20, 21, 29
Grace Commission, 21, 22, 32
Grace, Chairman J. Peter, 22

H

helpers, 9, 11, 12
highly trained, 11
Hoover Administration, vii, 2
Hoover, President Herbert, 3, 4, 9
House Subcommittee on Labor Standards, 18

I

inflation, 7, 35
interest groups, viii, 16, 24

investment in human capital, 12

J

journalistic pieces, 16

K

kick-back, 3

L

labor laws, 15
Labor Secretary, 4, 8, 17
labor standards, vii, ix, 1, 2, 6, 7, 33
laborers, ix, 2, 5
labor-protective statutes, 2
"little Davis-Bacon" acts, ix, 22, 36
local market wages, 12
locally prevailing wage, vii, 2, 3, 10-12, 19
lower-wage jobs, 13

M

manpower, 11, 32
mechanics, ix, 2, 5
minimum wage, ix, 1, 2, 5, 12, 27, 29, 31
minorities, 13, 31
minority and women workers, 11, 12
minority-owned businesses, 11
Morrall, John, 20, 21

N

national emergency, vii, 9
New Deal, 1, 7, 34
Nixon, President Richard, vii, 7, 31

O

Office of Management and Budget (OMB), 8

organized labor, 3, 36
overtime pay, 1, 2
overtime, 1, 2

P

payroll reports, vii
per diem, 2
Philips, Peter, 22
pick-up crews, 12
predetermination, 3, 5
private agencies, 17
private sector, 1, 2, 18, 21, 25, 32, 33
public construction, 12, 22
public contracting policy, 15
public employees, 2
public materials, 16
public project, 3
public sector, 16

Q

quality, 12, 20, 23, 29

R

Reagan Administration, viii, 18, 21
Reagan Labor Department, 8
Reagan reforms, 9, 18
Reagan, President, 8
Reischauer, Robert D., 18
Roosevelt Administration, 4
Roosevelt Subcommittee, 6

Roosevelt, President Franklin, vii, 4, 7
Roosevelt, Representative James, 6

S

safety, ix, 20
Secretary of Labor, ix, 3, 6, 9, 17
Subcommittee of the House Committee on Education and Labor, 6
subcontractors, 5
super minimum wage, 12
Supreme Court, 1, 26, 37
sworn affidavit, 4

T

taxpayer money, 12
trade union, 7, 23, 24
Truman Administration, 7

W

Wage appeals Board, 6
wage rate determination, 3, 6, 9, 12
wage rates, 2, 3, 5, 6
wage standards, 2
Walsh, Senator David, 5
West Coast Hotel v. Parrish, 1
White House, 3, 10
Wirtz, Willard, 6
women, 11, 12, 30